Words
OF WISDOM

Words OF WISDOM

**Those with wisdom will shine
as the brightness of the sky**

Book
No. 3

ROY MARTIN

Words of Wisdom

Copyright © 2021 by Roy Martin. All rights reserved.

No part of this publication may be reproduced, stored in a retrieval system or transmitted in any way by any means, electronic, mechanical, photocopy, recording or otherwise without the prior permission of the author except as provided by USA copyright law.

The opinions expressed by the author are not necessarily those of URLink Print and Media.

1603 Capitol Ave., Suite 310 Cheyenne, Wyoming USA 82001
1-888-980-6523 | admin@urlinkpublishing.com

URLink Print and Media is committed to excellence in the publishing industry.

Book design copyright © 2021 by URLink Print and Media. All rights reserved.

Published in the United States of America

Library of Congress Control Number: 2020922691
ISBN 978-1-64753-542-1 (Paperback)
ISBN 978-1-64753-543-8 (Digital)

10.02.21

Introduction

The scripture references are from the King James Version of the bible, with corrections of spelling of Old English words.

The words of wisdom for this book came from various sources; some from the bible, some from the authors personal experiences, some from "Old" sayings that contain a lot of wisdom, and some from insights to the author directly from God.

The words of wisdom in this book are in no particular order, so there are no chapters.

The author suggests that, if possible, you take this book with you so you can read it when you have to wait at the doctor's office, while riding a bus, etc. You may feel inclined to read it more than once.

Obviously, this is not an exhaustive study concerning wisdom. You can do your own research concerning wisdom, and make an appeal to God to provide you with wisdom.

It is understandable that some will disagree with what has been written in this book. The author respects your right to disagree.

1

As noted in Book No.1, wisdom is still the
principle thing, so get wisdom. But in your
getting, get also understanding. (Proverbs 4:7)

Satan is the father of lies according to John 8:44.
Does that mean he is the spiritual father of all liars?

If we want Jesus to answer our prayers, we should be
willing to obey his command that we love one another.

Admitting that you have a problem with sin
does not mean you are a failure. It means you
are honest, which is related to honor.

If you derive pleasure seeing those you hate suffer,
you need to find out what spirit you are.

If you believe God performs miracles,
some people will label you as crazy.

If you don't believe in miracles, then you would have
to believe those who wrote the bible are crazy.

Sometimes, you cannot trust people. Those that dance
at your wedding, may throw rocks at your grave.

If you want to know what war is like, talk
to those who have been in the trenches, not
those who have a theory about war.

If you receive a gift from someone that you knew
truly loved you, you would treasure that gift even
if it had little value. That is how love works.

Practicing safety begins in the mind.

Don't go to the grocery without a list if you
are hungry. Those are words for the wise.

God rewards obedience, not intelligence.

Take note of your compassion. It
tells you what drives you.

To a degree, you will be known according
to the company you keep.

You were not born in a box, so don't let someone put
you in a box where your thoughts are concerned.

Say to God, "Show me your glory." (Exodus 33:18-
19) You will need more than one day for God to
show you his glory. You will need a life time.

God yearns for us to seek an intimate
relationship with him.

Not knowing God's will is unwise according
to the bible. (Ephesians 5:17)

Guard your thinking. Your thoughts will
determine your destiny and your walk
toward your destiny. (Proverbs 23:7)

Our pride is smoke in God's nose. (Isaiah 65:5)

How can God be pleased when we delight in those
things that do not delight God? (Isaiah 65:12)

When you check yourself into a mental hospital,
rejoice. You are already on the road to recovery.

To the aged, time seems like it has wings.

Rebuke the unfruitful works of darkness, such as Halloween and secret societies. (Ephesians 5:11)

If you are God's servant, your steps are preordained. (Psalms 37:23)

If you are anointed by God, you can see what others cannot see. You will have wisdom that others do not have. (Proverbs 2;6)

Many people like having a savior, but they don't want their savior to be their boss, and definitely not their lord (their owner).

At some point you just have to let go of what you thought should happen and live with what is happening.

Everybody wants to be saved from the fires of hell, but they don't want to be saved from the sins they enjoy.

Jesus claimed to be the bread of life, and those that come to him will never hunger again. (John 6:35)

The bible says to do the work of God, and believe that Jesus is who he said he is. (John 6:28-29)

Teachers make a living by talking, but that does not mean the work is easy. It is an awesome responsibility. The number of people they can help is the same number they can hurt.

For a country to get healed, the healing will have to begin in God's house that is in that country. (2 Chronicles 7:14)

A soft answer turns away wrath. (Proverbs 15:1)

Husbands, say to your wife when she awakens in the morning, "Good morning, Beautiful." You will make her day, and yours also.

Remember, words are not like seeds, they are seeds. Whatever you sow(speak) is what you will reap. Sow seeds of strife, and you will reap strife.

It must surely grieve God's heart when his children believe he shows favoritism among his children by healing diseases in olden days but not in the present day.

Love is demonstrated by both our words and our actions. Husbands and wives, are you listening?

A word is not a word until it is spoken. A song is not a song until it is sung. However, it does not have to be out loud. You can speak and sing in your heart, and it will have an influence over you.

God is very bossy. If you don't like to be bossed, you won't like God.

To be a preacher of the gospel of the kingdom of God, you have to demonstrate the kingdom, not just preach the history of the kingdom. Those who see it demonstrated will have no excuse for refusing to believe your preaching when they see it demonstrated.

God said through the prophet Hosea, "My people are destroyed for a lack of knowledge." (Hosea 4:6) So, read the bible, the source of the knowledge of God.

It would be an act of wisdom on your part if you would pay close attention to the words you speak to yourself, because you will believe you before you will believe anyone else.

The bible says, "Taste the Lord and you will know he is good." But we cannot taste him if we do not trust him. (Psalms 34:8)

God redeems those who serve him, so vow to serve him. (Psalms 34:22)

Jesus is the King of kings, the Lord of lords, the Leader of leaders, and the Giver of givers.

Some people may not view God as their father who dishes out discipline. They may view him as their grandfather who dishes out the goodies. He actually does both.

To demonstrate the power of God's Holy Spirit, we must first demonstrate Jesus' compassion. (Matthew 14:14)

A fool has no delight in understanding. (Proverbs 18:2)

Husbands, when you have a spat with your wife, the way to get over it is to hold her tight. Give her a big bear hug.

Wisdom is shouting, "Hey, silly, how long are you going to stay silly?" (Proverbs 1:21-22)

Sometimes wisdom does not appear to be wisdom. Psalms 116:15 says, "Precious in the sight of God are the death of his saints." Obviously, God does not view our death the way we do.

Choose carefully the words you speak. You
can't call them back after you speak them.

Opposition provides you an opportunity
to shine brightly if you are correct.

You may have shame or fear of you past, but don't let
either deter you from who you are destined to become.

Don't desire to be exactly like another
person. God made you an original.

It would be an act of wisdom on your part to
respect people's right to disagree with you.

If one of Satan's followers criticizes you, take it
as a compliment if you are a follower of Jesus.

It is folly to answer a matter before you
have all of the details. (Proverbs 18:13)

A fool's mouth is his destruction. (Proverbs 18:7)

If we love physical pleasure more than we love
God, God views us as traitors. (2 Timothy 3:1-4)

God expects the church to be the church, not just do church. To know what this involves, study the book of Acts, and imitate that church.

Darkness and light are both the same to God. So, don't think you can hide your ungodly behavior under the cover of darkness. (Daniel 2:22)

Manage your life wisely by managing your time wisely. Lost time cannot be called back. However, God can restore your losses if you are his servant.

It is required of stewards that they be found faithful in their assignment. (1 Corinthians 4:2)

Don't tell God how much you love him unless you are willing to demonstrate that love toward others.

How wonderful would it be if the spirit of Christmas prevailed all year long, rather than the spirit of Halloween? The spirit of giving rather than the spirit of getting.

Honor and pride are not the same thing. Don't be prideful and call it honor. Pride has to do with feelings. Honor has to do with commitment.

The one who qualifies as the spiritual head of the household is the one who is the quickest to forgive wrongs.

God's glory is his goodness. His goodness is his grace and mercy. (Exodus 33:18-19)

Sometimes the pressures we feel are self inflicted, so don't blame others for all the pressures you feel.

The bible says there is a time to grab and a time to loose. What is this trying to tell us? It is like children coming to a point in life when they have to be willing to let go of their security blanket and use their hands to grab those things that are necessary for a fulfilled life. (Ecclesiastes 3:1-6)

Our personal testimonies concerning our experiences with God usually arise from the trials and tests that we went through on our way to having a personal relationship with God.

Satan's scheme is to make us robots that are programmed to serve him. God sets before us choices and gives us the right to choose. However, we cannot choose the consequences of our choices. The consequences are built into and become a part of our choices. So it would be wise to make the right choices. (Proverbs 18:21)

Get grounded in God's word. Then you will be prepared to run life's race, and finish without regrets.

Those mentioned in Acts 2:1-4 had a breakthrough anointing. The entire present day church started that day, because of the anointing. Check your church to see if it still has the Acts 2:1-4 anointing.

The bible says, "Delight yourself in the LORD and he will give you the desires of your heart." The word "delight" was translated from a word that has an idiom that means "soft and pliable". So this could have been translated this way, "Be soft and pliable in the hands of the LORD and he will give you the desires of your heart." (Psalms 37:4)

2

The bible says those that win souls are wise. (Proverbs 11:30) Now is your big chance to become wise.

God cannot always do what pleases himself. He is bound by the words he has spoken in the past. (Exodus 32:13-14)

God is a singer. He is the chief singer. (Habakkuk 3:1,19)

Without wisdom from God, we might make decisions that are not pleasing to God.

Even if your father and mother forsake you, you will not be a orphan if you accept God as your father and your provider. (Psalms 27:10)

When reading the bible, it is critical that you take note of which words were inspired by God and which words were written by the inspiration of a man. (Job 42:4-6)

> If you have not repented to God for your sins, your sins are terminal. The end result of sin is death. Not death of your body, but death of your spirit, which means you end up in hell when your body dies. (Romans 6:23)

How do you live in peace when those around you prefer conflict? You need to make a commitment to be a follower of Jesus so he can supply you with peace, his peace. (John 14:27)

> People without a worthwhile life will probably criticize your life.

In the garden of Eden, Eve did not see Satan as a snake. If she had she would have run from him. What she experienced was a voice that was very charming, and so will you. Be aware of this. Be prepared to rebuke it, or run for life.

> You would be wise not to take on more projects than you can handle. There comes a time when you have to say "NO".

The more wisdom you have, the more patience you will have. So, if you need more patience, strive for more wisdom.

Don't focus on your problems, focus on the solutions to your problems, which is knowledge of God's word. God knows the solution to everybody's problems, even a nations problems. (2 Chronicles 7:14)

Praising God is a weapon we can use to defeat demons, and defeat people who are being controlled by demons.

As far as we can tell, animals don't plan their future. So, man is not just another animal, even though he sometimes acts like one.

If you have family or friends who have not made a commitment to serve God, pray that the Lord of the harvest will send laborers into their life. (Matthew 9:38)

In their relationship with God, some people are like the lady who cleaned her house before the cleaning woman came because she did not want the cleaning woman to see all of that dirt in her house.

Compassion can be tormenting if you cannot resolve the problems that are involved in whatever you are compassionate about.

Doing a good deed toward others will make your heart smile.

God has made us a solemn promise, "Call unto me and I will show you great and mighty things that you don't know about." (Jeremiah 33:3)

There are many books, but there is a special book in heaven called THE BOOK OF LIFE. Your goal should be to have God write your name in that book. (Revelation 3:5)

Do not be deceived by the company you keep. Those who don't have faith in God may corrupt your faith in God's word. (1 Corinthians 15:33)

If you seek advice on managing money, you would be wise to seek out someone whose pay check is dependent upon him being right. Don't seek advice from someone on a set salary, who could be wrong 100% of the time and never miss a pay check.

Saving people from going to hell is serious business. It requires as much commitment as working in a business.

Feel with your heart and think with your head. Don't get these two reversed.

Some people will try to take advantage of your kindness, and try to use it to benefit their selfishness.

The Devil doesn't care who or what you worship as long as you don't worship the true God.

If you are not grounded in God's words, you will be subject to Satan's words. But you may not know those words came from Satan, because he is a deceiver, a master deceiver.

If you want to experience heaven on earth, do things God's way on earth. (Isaiah 55:9)

If God is true to his word, you would be wise to accept him as your God, because he has promised to never forsake you. (Deuteronomy 31:6; Hebrews 13:5)

God has a plan for your life, but so does the Devil. Whose plan you will follow is your choice.

Every religion claims to have the truth. But Jesus said,
"I am the truth." If Jesus told the truth, we cannot
know the truth unless we know Jesus. (John 14:6)

We need patience when we run the
race of life. (Hebrews 12:1)

In the Bible, brothers are those men who have
the same spiritual father. Jesus never referred
to those whose spiritual father was Satan as
his brothers, even if they were Jews.
(John 8:44)

Wisdom that is not used or not used properly becomes
corrupted. This is what caused Satan's downfall.
(Ezekiel 28:17) We can learn from Satan's failure.

The farmer who plows, plows in the hope of having a
bountiful harvest. So should we where our relationship
with God is concerned.(1 Corinthians 9:10)

You are more apt to change a person
who is misbehaving by honoring him
instead of exchanging insults.

The Bible admonishes us to trust in God with all
of our heart, not halfheartedly. (Proverbs 3:5)

Your honor toward people is what gives you access to their most inner feelings and counsel. Wives, you will never gain access to your husband's inner heart until you show him honor.

If you are not willing for God to put his name on you, he cannot bless with an abnormal blessing. (Numbers 6:22-27)

Since no one is perfect, God has figured out how to use imperfect people to get his word to us. So, don't get offended when imperfect people tell you about God. Compare what they say with what is written in the Bible.

The way we perceive will be the way we will receive. If you perceive a person is a liar, you will not believe anything he says about a perfect God.

Those to whom God has given much, much will be required of them. This is why Moses was not allowed by God to enter the country that God promised the Israelites. (Deuteronomy 32:49-52; Luke 12:4)

God's miracles have a voice. (Exodus 4:8) If you listen closely, his miracles will speak to you.

You don't have to like people to love them.
To like is a feeling. To love is a choice.

Hindsight is always 20/20 vision.

If an enemy curses you or lies about you, don't take it personally or try to get revenge. Forgive them and God will handle the revenge. (Hebrews 10:30)

You would be wise to view temptations as a heavy burden you have to carry, maybe for the rest of your life; unless you exchange your burden with Jesus, whose burden is light. (Matthew 11:28-30)

Joining a church will not save you from the fires of hell. You must believe that Jesus died for your sins and arose from the grave.(Romans 10:9)

Unresolved grief will adversely affect your relationship with God. Ask God to help you deal with your grief, not just one time, keep asking until he answers. (Luke 18:7)

Those who are great lovers of God, make great soldiers in God's army, because they have a cause to fight for.

Deception can sometimes be comfortable, even pleasureful. It can also be a trap that Satan uses to gain followers, but the day of reckoning will come in due time.

Pastors, if you are a good shepherd, you will risk your life to protect the sheep. (John 10:11-12)

There is a time and a place for everything under the sun. A time to be born and a time to die. A time to get and a time to give. A time to speak and a time to listen, etc. (Ecclesiastes 3:1-8)

Pride can masquerade as humor. Remember, God hates pride. He doesn't merely dislike it, he hates it. Pride is so powerful it caused the downfall of one of God's highest angels.

Be aware that anything you are attracted to has the potential to cause you to worship it instead of God.

If God utterly detests an idol made of gold or silver, would he detest it less if it was make out of chocolate? (Deuteronomy 7:26)

Many people have no conception of
heaven and hell because they have no
conception of how long eternity lasts.

It would be an act of wisdom if you would accept
the fact that the LORD GOD is the true God, the
faithful God, the God who honors his covenant of
grace and mercy toward those who honor him.

Do you have more patience with animals
than you do with people? If so, why?
Which one is make in God's image?

We are apt to make poor choices in life if
we don't comprehend how short our life
on earth is, and how long eternity is.

It has been proven scientifically that continuous strife
will adversely affect your physical and mental health.
Could this be the reason the Bible says it is an honor
for a man to cease from strife? (Proverbs 20:3)

You cannot laugh and be depressed at the same time.
So, when you are depressed, and don't know what is
causing it, seek something humorous, or think about
some humorous event that you have experienced.

You will not experience death if you believe that Jesus is the only begotten son of God, that he died for you, and that he arose from the grave. (John 11:25-26)

Just because your life style pleases you doesn't mean it is pleasing to God.

Seeing history in the making will not bring you any comfort when you are on your death bed, but scriptures you have memorized will bring you comfort. They will speak to you without you trying to rehearse them in your mind. That is part of God's promise to never leave us nor forsake us. (Deuteronomy 31:6)

Faith in God requires focus. Faith in anything requires focus. When we focus on Jesus, we no longer have a veil over our face. (2 Corinthians 3:13-18)

If you don't understand what you read in the Bible, read it out loud. The angels understand it, and they are obligated to bring it to pass when they hear it. (Psalms 103:20)

Your time is just as important to you as the things you possess. Be aware that people and events will sometimes rob you of your time. Time lost can never be called back.

Knowledge is essential, but we need wisdom in order to know how to use knowledge properly.

You will know you are God's child when you have an overwhelming desire to do whatever pleases his heart, and you desire to avoid those things that grieve his heart.

Bitterness is like an armed bandit. It will chase after you and steal your happiness.

God has promised his faithful servants that they will be the head and not the tail, they will be above and not beneath. (Deuteronomy 28:13)

A shepherd feeds his sheep pasture, from the word "pasture" comes the word "pastor'. God's shepherd feeds God's sheep knowledge and understanding. (Jeremiah 3:15)

Without forgiveness there would be no gospel. Without forgiving and being forgiven, there would be no good news, no gospel.

Look at your past only long enough to learn from it. Your hope is in your future, not in your past.

For daily bread from God, we must have daily
contact with God. Remember, God's word is God.
(John 1:1)

A sacrifice to God cannot be used as a substitute
for our obedience to God. (1 Samuel 15:22)

If you are God's servant, the battles you fight are
actually God's battles. And God is responsible
for the outcome. (Zechariah 2:8; Psalms 23:5)

If you know you are guilty concerning something,
don't pray for justice, pray for mercy. And show mercy
toward those who have wronged you. (Romans 11:31)

God does not love you because of what you
have done for him. He loves you because
he chose to love you. (John 3:16)

3

God does not just want to speak directly to you, sometimes he chooses to speak to you through other people. However, you should always compare what you hear to what the bible says, because Satan wants to speak to you also.

We may say that God is our king, but our actions may reveal that he is not our king.

To be God's servant, don't be concerned about your abilities. Focus on your availability, this is what God is looking for.

Not believing that Jesus is who he says he is, is a sin. (John 16:8-9)

Expectation is huge in God's realm, as well
as in man's realm. Ask any inventor how
many things he has invented accidentally.

If you don't love, your faith won't work in
the Kingdom of God. (Galatians 5:6)

When you get involved in performing God's miracles,
you will find out why Jesus referred to his miracles as
"work". It could also be compared to war. (John 9:4-7)

In your relationship with God, there
is no substitute for obedience.

As you read portions of the bible that you don't like,
you may find yourself getting closer to God; or it
may cause you to feel uncomfortable. Some people
like God better when he stays beyond their reach.

No one can remain neutral in the presence of blood,
and probably don't know why. (Leviticus 17:11)

You have two persons in you that want to rule
over you, your flesh and your spirit. You decide
which one will rule over you. (Romans 8:5)

When you become a new person by believing
that Jesus is who the bible says he is, Jesus will

give you a new name. Your new name will be "Chosen". No one but you will know that you have received this new name. (Revelation 2:17)

Give God your best, then you will have the right to believe that God will give you his best.

To be successful in performing miracles in God's kingdom, we must first believe that God's kingdom is worth fighting for. God's kingdom suffers violence. We have to become violent and take it by force. (Matthew 11:12)

If you want to change your world, change your thinking. You become what you think. You go where your mind takes you.

When you play tricks on people, you partner with the Devil. He is a master trickster.

God's glory is identified with a person, not a place; not even with clothing, as it was in the Old Testament era.

Be forewarned that lust can masquerade as love.

Think of eternal death as eternal darkness. You never see a sunrise or a sunset.

Don't let the Devil substitute humor for miracles.

God, your maker, thinks of himself as a husband would think toward his bride. A wayward bride breaks his heart. (Isaiah 54:5)

God occupies the praises of those who praise him. So, if you want to bring God on the scene, praise him.

Your body is listening to everything you say. Your words are seeds, and your body is the ground where the seeds are sown. So, be very selective in the seeds you sow. (Matthew 13:18-23)

Life is not just something to be endured, but to be enjoyed. Say to God, "No fear here." (John 14:27)

It is difficult to have patience when you are in pain. Use Jesus' name to rebuke whatever is causing the pain.

God loves it when we speak his words back to him. Speaking God's words causes us to focus on God and his words. (Isaiah 43:26)

To be a child of God, we must be willing to be led led by the Spirit of God. (Romans 8:14)

If you want to be truly free, invite God into every area of your life, including your past memories.

God cannot give us hope if we refuse to give him our disappointments and fears.

Don't be so proud that you think you are too good to be influenced by demons. Even Jesus had to contend with Satan. (Matthew 4:1-4)

Do not form a partnership with fear, or else it will become your bosom buddy. Dump your fears in God's lap by telling him that is what you are doing. (1 Peter 5:7)

Woe unto those who strive with their Maker. (Isaiah 45:9)

Our problems arise when we are attracted to the created more than the Creator.

If you are a cowboy, think of Jesus as being the smartest dude on the ranch.

Why do we live our lives in such a way as to give the impression that we believe we will live on earth forever?

Are you struggling with the pain of your past? Jesus said, "Come unto me and I will give you rest." Say, "Jesus, I come unto you. Give me rest." (Matthew 11:28-30)

When we love the earth more than we love God, God becomes jealous. (Nahum 1:2)

When you read the bible, don't be surprised if you hear a voice saying, "This is the way, walk in it." (Isaiah 30:21)

It is much easier to love someone if they love you first. (1 John 4:19)

Revenge is a marriage killer.

Game changers can improve your game or take you out of the game, depending on how you handle it, and how well you are anchored in God's words.

Thinking negative thoughts produce negative consequences.

Everybody wants to be loved, but everybody does not want to do the loving.

Don't be surprised if your fears give Satan an opportunity to come into your life. Satan is an opportunist. To deal with your fears, memorize Second Corinthians 10:5, and quote it when you have fearful imaginations.

Jesus died saving your life. (Romans 5:8)

When reading the bible, pay close attention to details, like you would if you were reading a recipe to make your favorite cake.

If you get offended by someone else's problems, you are doing their suffering for them.

Run from alcoholic beverages and narcotics. The good feeling they afford will eventually cease. Then they will get you down and stomp you.

Little is much when God is in it. (Proverbs 9:11)

The grace that taught you to fear God is the same grace that will relieve you of your fear of God.

Every time you quote scripture from the bible, you are returning God's words to him and calling to him. (Psalms 91:15; Isaiah 55:11)

There is no fervor like religious fervor.

Many people don't want to hear the truth about themselves, but they are eager to hear the truth about others.

If you want God to hear your words, talk to him morning, noon and night. (Psalms 55:17)

Which influences you the most, God's words or people's words? Which should influence you the most? Which contains the most wisdom?

It will require wisdom to know if a friend is a true friend. Their words toward you may be as smooth as butter, but behind their back they are loading their gun. (Psalms 55:21)

In the spiritual realm, a sworn oath is always based on the name of someone higher in authority than the person doing the swearing. When God swore an oath, he did not have anyone higher in authority, so he had to swear by his own name. (Hebrews 6:13)

If you are at a point in your life when your life seems like pieces of a jigsaw puzzle, ask God to help you find the pieces for each piece of the puzzle. (Isaiah 42:16)

If you are at war with yourself, stop it. You can stop it by focusing on Jesus, who has sworn to provide you with peace. (John 14:27)

There is no substitute for experience, whether in man's realm or God's realm. Experience will usually require you to get beyond your comfort zone.

You cannot be lazy and still expect to serve God. (Romans 12:11)

Be swift to hear and slow to speak, then you will be less apt to become angry. (James 1:19)

When God fills your cup, don't be surprised if it runs over. The overflow is God's blessing. (Psalm 23:5)

God watches to see how we handle crumbs and leftovers. (Matthew 15:22-28; John 6:12-13)

A word of wisdom to single men who want to get married. Be cautious about marrying a girl who can beat you at arm wrestling.

If faith is difficult for you to understand, think of it as trust.

A bribe will even blind the eyes of someone who is wise. (Deuteronomy 16:19; 1 Samuel 12:3)

Doing what you know is displeasing to God is like sticking your finger in God's eye.

You have only one life to live on earth, don't waste any of it. Don't live by emotions, live by purpose, a worthwhile purpose.

The real you is a spirit. Your body will some day die and return to dust from which it came. When it does, your spirit will have to leave the earth. You need to decide before your body dies where you want your spirit to spend eternity, either heaven or hell.

When trying to figure out why people do what they do, always take into account their level of maturity, but also make an allowance for the way they were raised.

There are three types of people in the world. There are those that make things happen. There are those that watch things happen. There are those who don't know what is happening. Can you figure which group you are in?

Do you dare ask God if he is pleased with your lifestyle?

Temptations will test your faith in God.
Allow your patience to help you resist the
temptations. Patience requires you to wait, and
temptations don't like to wait. (James 1:3-4)

When God's Spirit is with you, even darkness
will seem like light. (Psalms 139:11-12)

There is nothing wrong about disagreeing with
God and telling him so. But you must disagree
respectfully. Moses did, and God changed his mind
as to what he had planned to do. (Exodus 32;9-14)

Do not fear the supernatural, whether it involves
God or Satan. The more you experience Satan's
supernatural, the easier it is to accept God's
supernatural, as well as the spiritual world in general.

When you experience a blessing from God, you will also experience a good feeling. That is part of the reason for the blessing. Your feelings are important to God. It is what the bible calls joy.

God is closer to you than you realize. He is just a breath away. The bible says to call on him, and he will answer, "Here I am."(Isaiah 58:9)

If you will accept the true God as your God, his Spirit will come and dwell in your body. If you accept the false god as your god, his spirit will come and dwell in your body. (Romans 8:15)

Do you just eat your favorite dessert, or do you make love to it? This might reveal to you where your passion lies.

If you wait until everything is perfect in your life before you help people, you will never help them because things in your life will never be perfect.

Ponder this question, "Who is steering your hearing?" There are a lot of voices in the world demanding to be heard. (Luke 23:23-24)

Our goal should be that we will get close enough to God to hear his heart beating.

It may not be wise to share your dreams and your problems with just anybody. Some people can't handle your dreams, and some can't solve your problems in reaching your dreams.

Stay sober. Be vigilant. Your adversary, Satan, walks around like a roaring lion seeking someone to devour. (1 Peter 5:8) A roaring lion is a hungry lion. A lion with his belly full doesn't roar, he sleeps.

Unless God builds the house, those that build it labor in vain. (Psalms 127:1)

Wisdom requires truth. Do not expect to be wise if you do not whole heartedly embrace the truth, including the truth about yourself.

The bible says we are more than conquerors if we love God. What would be more? After we tear down Satan's kingdom in our life, we need to build God's kingdom in our life. This would be more than just being a conqueror.

Fools despise wisdom, because it exposes their foolishness. (Proverbs 1:7)

Cling to God and he will cling to you. You cling to God by clinging to his word. (John 1:1; Psalms 63:8)

When God is not your God, you will always
be right in your own eyes. (Judges 21:25)

Yours fears can be as harmful to you as your enemies.

Blood has a voice. Innocent blood we shed on
purpose will talk to us, maybe in the wee hours
of the night. To get free of the voice, repent of the
shedding of the innocent blood. (Genesis 4:10)

In olden days people worshipped God in a
building called a Temple. In the present day
the worshippers themselves are the temple. In
olden days God put his name in the Temple.
In the present day God puts his Spirit in the
worshippers. (1 Kings 9:3; 1 Corinthians 3:16)

How can you expect to please God if you are not
willing to change to conform to his word?

If God can cause a dumb donkey to speak words
of wisdom, surely there is hope for you and me to
speak words of wisdom. (Numbers 22:20-30)

Not only swear worthwhile promises to God,
swear worthwhile promises to yourself.

When you are praying to God and telling him what is on your heart, don't forget to ask him what is on his heart.

Loving is not when you get, loving is when you give. (John 3:16)

We can see faults in others much quicker than we can see faults in ourselves.

When you read in the bible what Jesus says, you cannot remain neutral. You will want to hug him or hit him. Read the books in the bible called MATTHEW, MARK, LUKE and JOHN; and see how they affect you. Get a bible where Jesus' words are printed in red and read the red.

Loving God usually begins by loving his word, and loving his name enough that you want to obey him. (1 John 5:3)

You would be wise to avoid strife, even among your family members. In the bible, strife is on the same list as adultery concerning things we are to avoid. Strife will rob you of God's gifts of love, joy, peace, patience, kindness, goodness, faith, gentleness and self-control. (Galatians 5:19-23)

Spiritual light has power, but so does
spiritual darkness. (Colossians 1:13)

Love of money could cause some people to
become killers. If it does not kill people,
it can certainly kill relationships.

Memorizing bible scriptures voluntarily is
proof of your love for God and his word.

When you are lying on your bed of affliction, your
memory of the jokes you heard in the past will
not bring you any comfort. What will bring you
comfort is the bible verses you have memorized.

Religion was developed by men to get to God.
God's method to get God to men was developed
by God. God's word is the method God uses to
accomplish this. God's word became flesh and
dwelled among men. Our part in this is to believe
and receive the word that became flesh. (John 1:1,14)

We cannot hide from God, but we can
hide from ourselves if we are deceived.

Hold God so close that you can hear his
heart beat, and he can hear yours.

Experiencing church is not the same as experiencing God's glory, his grace and mercy. (Exodus 33:18-19)

When you pray, don't say, "God, if you do such and such, then I will do such and such." Rather, use the word "when" instead of "if". It confirms your faith in God answering your prayer.

The blind can't lead the blind. So don't expect someone who is not filled with God's Spirit to instruct you on how to get filled with God's Spirit.

God will not only help you dream your dream of destiny, he will help you fulfill your dream.

It brings joy to God's heart when he hears his children call him Father or Daddy or Poppa. It is a violation of Jesus' teachings to call a physical man our spiritual father. (Matthew 23:9)

If you are God's servant, and you ask him to help you solve a certain problem, don't be surprised if he gives you a solution that is illogical, and may even appear to be stupid. (Joshua 6:1-5)

A temptation to sin against God is not the only temptation we face. We can be tempted to stop serving him because he does not respond to our prayers as soon as we thought he should. Abraham had to wait ten years for the son to be born that God promised him.

It is both humbling and exciting when we believe that we are made in the image and likeness of God. And that he has entrusted us to have dominion over all his creation except other people, who are also made in his image and likeness. (Genesis 1:26)

It is comforting to know that when we have a multitude of problems, God's servants can trust God to intervene in our behalf. (2 Chronicles 20:15)

Those who have made a decision to believe that Jesus is who he says he is, and have confirmed their belief by being baptized, qualify to have God's Spirit as their comforter and prayer partner. (Romans 8:26; John 14:26)

God is not only a king, he is the King of kings. (Revelation 19:16)

Since Jesus' other name is Word, the more we talk about him, the more real he becomes to us. The reverse of this is also true. The less we talk about him, the less real he is to us. (John 1:14; Revelation 19:13)

Even though they are not orphans, some people have an orphan spirit that makes them feel like an orphan. God wants to be a father to the fatherless, but the fatherless have to accept him as their father. (Psalm 37:4-5)

The man that is more foolish than a fool is the man that is conceited in his wisdom. (Proverbs 26:12)

People will hate you for telling the truth if they don't want the truth known. (Amos 5:10)

The most deceptive praise is when we praise ourselves and don't even realize it.

Racism is a two-way street. No one has a monopoly on racism.

Even if you lose the game, you need to continue to have a winning attitude. It will stand you in good stead for future events. So, continue to serve God even during the times you fall short. God will view you as a champion.

When you quote the good words that someone has spoken, you honor that person. So, learn as much as you can about what Jesus has spoken. Quote it to yourself and to others.

Have you ever wondered how God sees us? Would it surprise you to know that God doesn't look on our exterior, he looks on our heart. (1 Samuel 16:7)

Just think of how many arguments you could win if you could make you voice sound like thunder. This is how God wins all of his arguments. (Job 40:9) This is probably why we raise our voices when we get in an argument.

When laboring for God, it is better to try and fail than to not try at all. God rewarded Noah for preaching even though he never won any converts.

Judging is not the same as condemning, even though the translators of the bible used the words interchangeably in the King James Version of the bible. Jesus judged the woman as an adulteress in John 8:11, but he never condemned her. Why would Jesus tell her to sin no more unless he judged her as a sinner?

Whatever your passion is, it will drive you like a task master with a whip.

Whatever the words are that are in your heart in abundance will come out through your mouth, sometimes without you even thinking about them. (Matthew 12:34)

If you are Jesus' servant, he has offered to
be your servant. (John 13:5,12-16)

Sometimes, we can get a fuller understanding of a scripture in the bible when we consider what the opposite would be. Psalms 86:12 says, "I will praise you, O God, with all my heart." The opposite would be, "I will praise you, O God, with part of my heart."

Could it be that God wants you to tithe your income to him because he wants your heart? Jesus said wherever your money is, is where your heart will be. (Matthew 6:21)

Could it be that some people don't love God is because they don't know God, they only know about him?

For God to be pleased with us, we must return unto him and serve him with all of our heart and all of our soul. (Deuteronomy 30:2)

If you know Jesus personally, he will set you free from religion just like he set free from religion a man in the bible named Saul. (Acts 9:1-16)

There are two types of love. The love that you give and the love that you get. Both have a blessing, but the love you give will bless you the most. (Acts 20:35)

Believing in God is not the same as believing God, believing what he says. Even Satan believes in God. (James 2;19)

We are saved from the fires of hell by hope, but hope that is seen is not hope. Hope involves the future, which means we must have patience to acquire what we are hoping for. (Romans 8:24-25)

5

Be aware that God can read your mind. (Hebrews 4:12) So, cast down every thought that exalts you above God. (2 Corinthians 10:5)

Saying, "The Lord is my shepherd" is the same as saying, "The Lord is my boss." Remember that the next time you quote the twenty-third Psalm.

Don't over analyze the bible. Don't expect to have full knowledge of the bible the first time you read it. Much of the bible involves word pictures as well as parables, allegories, and metaphors.

Invite God into every room of your house and every room of your heart.

Make it your goal to progress in your bible reading to the point you can make this vow to God "God, if you will reveal yourself to me as I read the bible, I will serve you for the rest of my life."

Forgive yourself when you mess up. This is better than making excuses for your mess.

If your words have power, you could say your words have muscle. Muscle can build up or tear down, and so can your words. It was with words that God created the world. (Genesis 1:1-3)

If you hide your personality in a closet, the closet will become your prison. Closets can be used for praying, but should never by used for hiding your personality. (Matthew 6:6)

When the Devil threatens you, rejoice; because you are a threat to his kingdom.

If you are not prepared to be extremely blessed by God, his blessing can be overwhelming. (Luke 5:3-8)

Don't put off until tomorrow what you can do today. Tomorrow will have its own tasks to do.

You can offer your help to anyone, any time. But be cautious when it comes to offering advice.

Having God's presence with you is the same as having God with you, even though you can't see him. (Exodus 33:14)

Don't just think your prayer to God, speak it. Speaking puts legs on your prayers.

The financial world has its own golden rule. They believe that whoever has the gold makes the rules.

Refusal to fear when confronted by the Devil is proof to the Devil that you are not afraid of him. But the only way you can do that is to have the power of God's Spirit in you. (Luke 11:13)

A pessimist will believe he should be thankful for bad luck, because if it wasn't for bad luck he would not have any luck at all.

If you depend on your taste to tell you whether or not something is good, taste God and you will know he is good. (Psalms 34:8)
We taste his goodness when we trust him.

How do you view God? Do you even believe there is a God? Your relationship with God is determined by how you view him.

We can't love like God loves unless we have his Spirit residing in us, because love is one of his "fruits". (Galatians 5:22-23)

The greatest revelation you can have is the revelation that God truly loves you.

We take on the nature of who we believe. If we believe God, we take on his nature. If we believe Satan, we take on his nature. This is what happened to Eve in the garden of Eden. She chose to believe Satan rather than God, and ate the forbidden fruit. She passed some of that fruit on to Adam, and he ate it. (Genesis 3:1-6)

Read the bible. It will provide you with information that will give you inspiration that will bring about transformation. (2 Corinthians 5:17)

Be aware that some church hymns are not according to the bible. A Christmas tree did not proclaim Jesus' birth, good will toward men and peace on earth. Neither did Jesus' cross cause us to see light. The bible says God's word brings light. (Psalms 119:105,130)

You can be full of Christian religion and still be scripturally illiterate. To please God, it is absolutely necessary that we stay grounded in his word. Jesus said to abide (live) in his word. (John 15:4)

Your soul will always be restless until it finds rest in the one who created it.

The most difficult thing to do is nothing and think nothing. It is difficult to be completely comfortable with complete silence. But stillness is necessary to hear God's voice with clarity. (Psalms 46:10)

You can't judge a book by its cover, even if it is very attractive. The same applies to judging people.

On Judgment Day don't expect to be able to save yourself, regardless of how strong you are or how intelligent you are.

When the Spirit of God takes up residence in you, impossibilities become possibilities. (Ephesians 1:19-20)

Seasons change in our lives, and we must be willing to change also, or we could get left behind. This includes such things as the loss of employment, the loss of a loved one, a divorce, etc.

Do you dare say to God, "I will go anywhere you want me to go if you will go with me."

Whether you believe it or not, whether you like it or not, your mind is a battleground of conflicting thoughts. Your spirit is the commanding general in the battle that is going on in your mind. If you are not grounded in God's word, your spirit will not know how to fight the battle.

After you forgive those who have wronged you, pray for them and ask God to bless them with something that will cause them to confess the error of their ways. (Luke 5:4-9)

The time will come when God will shake both the heavens and the earth. The only thing that will be left standing will be those things that cannot be shaken. (Hebrews 12:26-29)

When you "see" the invisible world with your "spiritual" eyes, you will feel more connected to it than the physical world. This is why the occult can be so attractive if you see it before you see God's kingdom, and can't make a comparison.

When we rub shoulders with God, he rubs shoulders with us. We don't have to do any work for this to happen. It is a gift. We don't have to earn a gift.

Don't depend on unhappy people to make you happy.

Don't try to defend yourself against Satan until you first submit yourself to God. This also applies to accusations by Satan's children here on earth. (John 8:44; James 4:7-8)

If you can't love the unlovely, love them with God's love, which is based on giving, not feelings. (John 3:16)

Have you ever wondered how big God is? The earth is his footstool. (Isaiah 66:1)

Suffering for God does not involves sickness. It involves waiting on God to fulfill his promises, especially when God haters taunt you when something doesn't happen as soon as you thought it would. Jesus' birth was prophesied many years before it happened, even those who prophesied it grew old and died before Jesus was born. (Isaiah 9:6-7)

When we run the race of life, we are tempted to focus on the prize we expect to receive. But the bible says to press toward the goal that qualifies us for the prize. (Philippians 3:14) In God's kingdom, the goal is being faithful servants. (Matthew 25:23)

Satan and his kingdom produce chaos. Jesus and his kingdom produce peace. (John 14:27)

Our knowledge of technology has increased, but it has not increased our contentment. (Daniel 12;4)

Those who do what Jesus did will draw people to Jesus. But to do what Jesus did, we must have on us what Jesus had on him, which was God's Spirit. (Luke 4:18)

Part of God's goodness is that he is true to his word; all of his word, not just the part we agree with.

What would have to happen for you to be convinced that God loves you? (John 3:16)

Sometimes sin is an inside job. No one knows about it but you. So it doesn't hurt anyone but you. Yet, it still needs to be repented of.

There is a risk of being so heavenly minded that we are no earthly good; but it is a risk we must take, and trust God to help us balance the two.

The true servant of God is afraid not to tithe. This is how you can tell if you actually fear God.

It is difficult to have an intimate relationship with God if we have a broken heart. Jesus is seated at the right hand of God and makes intercession for us, so ask him to pray that you will be healed of a broken heart. (Luke 4:18; Colossians 3:1; Romans 8:34)

It would be an act of wisdom on your part if you tolerate people when you don't agree with their beliefs or conduct. God gives all of us the right to believe whatever we want to believe; even though he warns us that all beliefs have consequences.

In reaching your goals in life, you will probably need help from others. So, stay connected to people.

Some people's beauty is in their personality.

If you become his servant, God will help you fight your battles. (Isaiah 49:25)

The battle against evil spirits was won by Jesus at the cross. If we connect with Jesus, we reap the rewards of that victory. (Colossians 2:15)

If you don't forgive those that wrong you, you will never have peace.

If God performs a miracle, he gets all of the glory. So, he must be willing to do all of the work that causes the miracle, even though we speak the words for the miracle.

The difference between wishing and hoping is that hope, bible hope, has substance that will cause what is hoped for to come to pass. That substance is faith. (Hebrews 11:1)

Don't harden your heart because someone has rejected you or criticized you. That will give them control over your emotions. You should be in charge of your emotions. (John 14:27)

If you feel comfortable serving God, you should be concerned. Jesus promised us rest and peace, but not comfort. Jesus said those who serve him will be persecuted if they do what he did during his earthly ministry, in the same manner he was persecuted. (John 15:20)

Our donations to the church are an abomination to God if our heart is not "right" with God. (Proverbs 21:27)

God is color blind, and he is blind to
people's outward appearance. He looks
on people's hearts. (1 Samuel 16:7)

It is difficult to stay neutral in the presence of blood,
especially our own blood. The bible says that life is
in the blood. God forbad the Israelites to eat blood.

Your "will" can be your best friend or your worst
enemy. You can say, "I will believe in miracles
according to God's word." Or you can say, "I
will not believe according to God's word. I will
only believe what I can see." (John 20:24-29)

God has promised that if we will serve him, he
will bless what we eat, what we drink, and take
sickness away from among us. (Exodus 23:25)

The plans you have for your life will be better
plans if God is involved. (Jeremiah 29:11)

6

If we wait until we feel worthy in order to experience God's kingdom, we will probably never experience it. In God's kingdom, we function by faith, not feelings. (Romans 1:17)

Those who choose to be God's servants are the wisest and greatest in God's eyes. Forced servants are slaves; therefore, they are not free. (Mark 9:35)

Some battles are not won by power alone, but by persistence and power.

Pleasure and contentment are not the same thing, but we are inclined to think they are. So, when we are discontented, we seek more pleasure.

It is not a coincidence that the bible refers to faith in God as a fight. We will encounter many forces that could cause us to lose our faith if we don't fight to keep it. (1 Timothy 6:12)

If you ask God a question, he will probably answer with a picture in words, or tell you a parable, which will be like a picture. (Luke 10:29-37)

The compassion that Jesus portrayed during his earthly ministry was not a religion, it resulted in love that helped people. (John 15:13)

The true God's other name is Love. (1 John 4:16)

If you want a bigger vision, think bigger.

Desiring to control people is a form of idolatry. So is expecting people to provide you with peace instead of God providing you with peace. (John 14:27)

You might have a god other than the true God, but you do not know it because you don't recognize it as your god. (Philippians 3:19)

If you please God, you can be sure you displease Satan. His persecution of you will be your confirmation that you have pleased God.

It is essential for us to abide (live) in Jesus if
we want to avoid the fires of hell. (John 15:16)
How do we do that? By living in his words. Jesus
and his words are the same. (John 1:1,14)

God must enjoy coming to earth and talking
to his children. Adam and Eve did not ask
God to come into the garden of Eden. He
did it of his own free will. (Genesis 3:8)

Jesus said during his earthly ministry that his words
were Spirit. (John 6:63) Jesus is now on earth as a
Spirit (Holy Spirit). To connect with him, we speak
his words back to him that are recorded in the bible.
(Proverbs 18:21; Isaiah 54:11; Matthew 11:28-30)

If God's words don't govern your life, don't be
surprised if your likes and dislikes are very similar
to an animal, tamed and untamed. You will live
by your senses. Your world will be the physical
realm. The real you is a spirit, but spiritual things
will seldom, maybe never, enter your mind.

Hey, Silly, how long are you going to stay
silly? (Proverbs 1:22) How long are you going
to refuse sound counsel? (Proverbs 1:28)

Can we be a child of God without being led by the Spirit of God? (Romans 8:14)

If people really knew how bad hell is, they would not want their worst enemy to go there. Jesus commands his followers to do good to those that hate God. Praying for their salvation would be doing them a favor, even if they don't appreciate you praying for them. You are not responsible for the way they respond to your good deeds toward them.

If Satan wants your opinion, he will give it to you.

Just like God's servants enjoy serving God, Satan's servants enjoy serving Satan; because he has deceived them into believing he is the true God.

Reading personal testimonies in the bible will inspire you if you are a servant of God. If you are not a servant of God, they may inspire to become a servant of God. (Psalms 119:111; Isaiah 54:17)

It is an awesome revelation to know God's Spirit, who raised Jesus from the dead, will dwell in us if we ask him. (Romans 8:11) He doesn't dwell in us partially, but in his fullness.

The bible says those that serve God are
of a different spirit than those that don't
serve God. (Numbers 14:24)

Do you dare dream God's dream. If so, let God
know it, even if he can read your mind.

Compromising on God's word is the same
as being disobedient to God's word.

Our disobedience toward God grieves
God's Spirit. (Ephesians 4:25-30)

To exercise faith in God, you must be able to focus
intently on the word of God, because that is where
our faith in God comes from. (Romans 10:17)

If you were the president of a Theological
Seminary, and you were needing some advice
in running the Seminary, would you consult
professionals or would you consult Theo,
the one the Seminary is named after?

If what you commit to God does not make you
weep or feel like weeping, you have not given to
God what is precious to you. (Psalms 126:6)

Kindness is contagious. Put it to
the test and see for yourself.

Dwell on your past mistakes only long
enough to make you determined not to make
the same mistakes again. Don't brood over
them. Don't make them members of your
family. Don't store them in your bosom.

God is a generous father, and he enjoys giving to
his children. So, become one of his children.
(Ephesians 4:8; 1 Timothy 6:17;
James 1:5; Luke 11:11-13)

Does this sound like wisdom: Give and it shall
be given unto you, good measure, pressed
down, shaken together and running over
shall men give unto you? (Luke 6:38)

Are you a giver, or do you continually think
about what others can do for you?

Compassion usually involves your hands. Lust usually
involves your eyes. This is how you can usually
distinguish compassion from lust. (1 John 2:16)

Have you ever wondered how many people would
miss you when you die? Have you ever wondered

why this is important for you to know? Could it be an indication as to how you have lived your life?

Allow God to perfect his love in you. It will cast out any fear you have. (1 John 4:18)

When God speaks anything to you, write it down in a journal or diary and date it. This will be your way of honoring God for giving you words of direction or words of wisdom, even if you don't understand all he is speaking.

Would you believe that you are on God's mind, and he has a plan for your future? (Jeremiah 29:11) Would you have more hope if you followed his plan? (1 Corinthians 2:9-10)

If God finds fault with you, that does not mean he condemns you. (John 8:3-11) God reserves condemnation for the end of the world. Until then, God points out our faults and admonishes us to do better so we won't be condemned with the rest of the world. (1 Corinthians 11:32)

Don't be discouraged if you are thrown in jail for serving God. God will continue to speak to you and tell you what to do. (Jeremiah 33:1)

Church Leaders, are you leading according to God's Spirit, or according to your own spirit?

Do you believe in free speech only for those who believe what you believe? That is not wisdom. That is just being bossy.

God's Spirit wants to become your closest friend, your bosom buddy. (James 2:23; Isaiah 40:10-11)

Would it be accurate to say we want to spend time with those we love? Would it be accurate to say you don't love God if you don't look forward to spending time with his Spirit, who Jesus says is your Comforter. (John 14:26)

Sometimes your closest family members will entice you away from serving God. That was a serious offence in Old Testament days. (Deuteronomy 13:6-11)

Before going to bed every night, ask God to guard you and give you a dream that will help you be a better servant. Have a pencil and paper nearby so you can record your dream as soon as you awaken. Don't forget to date it.

Many people have heard of Joshua's victory over the heavily fortified city of Jericho as recorded in the bible. (Joshua 6:1-2) But very few are aware of what God told Joshua to do to prepare for battle. (Joshua 1:8) If you have a battle to fight, ask God if you will have success if you have prepared the same way.

When you laugh, the whole world will laugh with you. When you cry, you will cry by yourself unless there is someone nearby with compassion. (John 11:33-35)

When you have made a commitment to serve God, don't look back, neither to the good nor the bad.

(Luke 9:62)

Don't become discouraged if God corrects you. It is better to be corrected by God than to be praised by Satan. (Proverbs 3:11)

The poorest people in the world are those that die without hearing the good news that God loves them, and they don't have to be afraid of death if they put their trust in God.

Forgiveness feels good coming toward you, but it may not when it is going from you toward others. But do it anyway. The rewards will come in due time.

Everyone has a right to be wrong, even if they don't know they are wrong. God gave us that right, starting with Adam and Eve. (Genesis 2:16-17)

Who wanted Jesus to be crucified? It wasn't the atheists, they couldn't find any fault in him. (John 19:11) It was those who claimed to be God's people. (John 19;11) It would be an act of wisdom on our part if we believe what Jesus said about himself. (John 18:37)

When we rebel against God's word, we are rebelling against God. (Psalms 107:11)

A word of wisdom for those who want to go to college: You probably will not use more than twenty percent of what you learn in college when you are employed. But you will not know in advance which twenty percent that will be, so learn all you can.

Daily contact with God is necessary for daily wisdom. Wisdom will be your daily delight. (Proverbs 8:1-4,30)

Don't forget to give thanks unto God for he is good and his mercy endures forever. (Psalms 118:29)

The writers of the bible said they were servants of God. However, Jesus said his followers were more than just servants, they were his friends. (John 15:15)

Pursue your dream with fervor, but be open to new dreams that come your way. (Psalms 37:4-5)

If you have made a commitment to serve God, and you refuse to forgive those who wrong you, you are being disobedient to God. (Matthew 18:21-22)

Nothing escapes God's attention. He even knows what you are thinking. (Psalms 139:1-2)

Some people love darkness more than light. Could it be because their deeds are evil? (John 3:19)

Don't be envious of the prosperous wicked. The more they get, the more they want. This will keep them from enjoying what they already have, because they focus on getting more and more. (Psalms 37:1)

The bible says King David was a man after God's own heart. The bible does not say if it was by accident or he had to work for it.

We were born to love, but we got perverted by Satan when he came on the scene. We were created in God's image, and God is love. (1 John 4:8)

No one can come to the Father (God) without coming through Jesus. God set it up that way, so we would have to honor Jesus, his only begotten son. (John 3:16-18)

God has many sons, but he has only one begotten son. The others come into God's family by adoption. (Ephesians 1:5)

Make sure your commitment to serve God is solid.

You can find out something about yourself by noticing how you treat animals, and compare it to how you treat people.

You are made out of dirt, and you will return to dirt when you die. (Genesis 3:19)

If you are not following Jesus, you are not one of his sheep. (John 10:3-4)

7

Harboring unforgiveness can cause you to
be mentally or physically sick if you make
a commitment to be obedient to God.

Be aware of what you spend your time thinking
about. If your thoughts are not pleasing to God,
cast them down by quoting 2 Corinthians 10:5.

If you want to have peace, you must not only
forgive others, you must also forgive yourself if
you have caused harm to others; even if the harm
was accidental. Even if it caused someone to die.

Be careful that you don't put a curse on yourself
by your words, such as "I wish I had never
been born." If you have done this, then repent
and ask God to forgive you. (Job 3:1-3)

You might have incurred occultic influences in your life if your ancestors were involved in occultic activity. Forgive your ancestors and rebuke in Jesus' name the demons that are coming against you, even if you have to speak the rebuke several times over several days. You will know when you are successful in driving the demons out of your life.

If you commit your life to God, he will give you a new song to sing. A song that will praise him. (Psalms 40:3)

Would you believe that the same Spirit that raised Jesus from the dead dwells in you if you have committed your life to serve God? (Romans 8:11)

When you are discouraged, don't become silent, become vocal. Call on the God who can bring you out of the pit of despair and set you upon a rock. (Psalms 40:2)

We can be both alive and dead. Alive in our body, but dead in our spirit. (Romans 8:10)

Secrecy and darkness in our dealings are of Satan. You are not a child of secrecy and darkness if you have committed yourself to serve God. (Ephesians 5:8-14) If your dealings are of God, shout it from the house tops. (Luke 12:3)

In order to come to God, you first have to believe he exists. Then you have to believe that he rewards those that diligently seek him. You don't have to find him to be rewarded, but you must seek him diligently. Notice the key word "diligently". (Hebrews 11:6) If you die before you find him, you will still be rewarded.

You have only one life to live, so make it count for something.

When we read God's word, we should hear trumpets calling us to battle Satan. If we don't prepare for battle, we will be defeated.

Don't die angry. Choose to die in peace, the kind of peace Jesus offers us. (John 14:27)

Every house has a foundation. Those who have received God's Spirit are now God's house. Their foundation is God's words. (Hebrews 3:6; 1 John 2:5)

Cast your cares upon God, then your cares become his cares. (1 Peter 5:7)

As strange as it might seem, the physical realm is controlled from the spiritual realm. God is a Spirit, and so are his angels. Satan is a spirit, and so are his angels. The controlling is done through words,

through speaking words. The evidence of this is
all throughout the bible, starting with the book
of Genesis. God said something seven times, and
God saw. What did he see? He saw what he said.

In the world, you will have turmoil. Get connected
to Jesus. He has overcome the world. (John 16:33)

When Jesus started his earthly ministry, he was first
anointed by God to preach the gospel of the Kingdom
of God. Then he demonstrated the Kingdom of God
by performing miracles. (Matthew 4:17; Acts 10:38)

If you feel like you are married to your purpose, you
are more apt to be successful in fulfilling your purpose.

> It is not enough to want to do the right thing.
> You have to know what to do that is the right
> thing to do. This is why we need to read in
> the bible what Jesus taught. (John 16:33)

If you want peace in your life, be quick to forgive
every offense, even if you don't feel like forgiving.

Church members, have you noticed in the
bible that when God asks someone to do
something, he never asks them if it is convenient

for them to do what he asks them to do?
Sometimes it can be very inconvenient.

Don't be tempted to do just barely enough to get by.
God rebuked the Israelites for bringing him offerings
that were less than their best. (Malachi 1:14)

Just because you went to night school doesn't mean
you can read in the dark. Just because you park
yourself on a church pew every Sunday doesn't
mean you can discern the forces of darkness.

The more time you spend reading the bible
concerning what Jesus taught, the more your
life will be transformed for the better.

If your doctor says you have cancer, don't say to
people, "I have cancer." Rather, say to people, " I
am fighting cancer." Your words have power. The
bible says you will have what you say. (Mark 11:23)

Good things are not always God things.
Don't get the two confused. For example,
cleanliness is not next to godliness.

Money will control you unless you
learn the purpose of money.

Jesus was sometimes so bold he could be considered as being rude. He invited himself to a man's house, according to Luke 19:2-5.

If you feel comfortable making excuses for your sins, that is proof that God's Spirit does not dwell in you. (John 8:9)

Don't believe every voice you hear in your mind. It would be wise to question it. (1John 4:1-6)

The church needs to preach Jesus' resurrection often. It will draw people to him according to John 12:32.

Can violence be used to promote peace? Maybe, if it is not for a selfish motive. (Matthew 21:12-13)

Those who walk in spiritual darkness, don't know where they are going. (John 12:35-36)

When a man is close to death and begins to reflect back on his life, it is doubtful he will say that he wishes that he had spent more time on his job and less time with his family.

You will probably have different feelings when money comes into your pocketbook than when it leaves your pocketbook.

The most difficult words to speak are,
"Please forgive me." You may have to literally
push the words out of your mouth.

When it comes to people to people relationships,
learn to bend and you will never be broken.

Some people have to almost die before they
learn how to live. You may be shocked to learn
that the world does not revolve around you.

Jesus said we are either for him or against
him. There is no middle ground. He forces
us to make a choice. (Luke 11:23)

The grass on the other side of the fence
will be greener if you devote the necessary
time to care for it and water it.

Husbands and Wives, try this: Each one pick
a separate week, and commit yourself to be
the other one's servant concerning doing and
listening. After the two weeks, sit down together
and analyze your marriage. Are you any wiser?

Everyone has pluses and minuses in their lives. Our
goal should be to have more pluses than minuses.

Sins are sometimes referred to in the bible
as being unclean, because that is the way we
feel when we become aware of our sins.

We not only need a revelation from God
of what we need to do to please him, we
need a deep revelation. (John 8:29)

Even psychologists who don't serve God
are beginning to realize the power of
forgiveness to heal broken hearts.

You have Jesus in your heart or Satan. There is no
such thing as being neutral, being your own person.

Some people fear Satan more than God, and that is
just the way Satan wants it to be. (Matthew 10:28)

Religion substitutes programs and procedures
for a personal relationship with God. We can
have these and still have a personal relationship
with God. So there is no need to substitute.

Whenever you do someone a favor who is having
a bad day, the effect of your favor is multiplied.

People are apt to revile and criticize what they don't understand, rather than investigating to see if what they don't understand has value or merit. (Jude 1:10)

Jesus has made available to us the keys we need to be a force in the Kingdom of God. One of those keys is to forgive those who have wronged us. (Matthew 18:21-22) There are other keys, but forgiving is probably the key that we will have the most difficulty using. (Luke 17:3-4)

If God is in your mouth (your words), he will be in your heart. If he is in your mouth only occasionally, he will be in your heart only occasionally. (Romans 10:8)

An important part of recovering from depression is to do other people a favor. Start with small favors, then gradually work toward larger favors, especially those favors that involve you spending money. The best place to start is favors toward your family members. (Acts 20:35)

If Satan can get your ear, he can eventually get your tongue. You will start making excuses for what you do wrong rather than repenting of it.

God is looking for people who will become fanatical for his kingdom, so they will eventually become movers and shakers in his kingdom. (Acts 17:1-6)

> Some people would like to have the power that Jesus had on the earth, but not his compassion. Power without compassion can become selfish, even dangerous.

> A riddle with wisdom: Why are we more cordial toward strangers than we are toward those of our own household?

> Your mouth is connected to your heart. If you have issues in your heart, they will be manifested in your mouth, your words.

Miracles performed in Jesus' name lend credibility to Jesus being raised from the dead. (John 16:23)

Our position in the Kingdom of God is in proportion to our devotion to God. (Matthew 10:7-8)

To be strong in God's truth, we have to know what his truth is. God's truth is his word. (John 17:17)

The most powerful weapon in God's kingdom is love. Not goose bump love, but God's love bestowed upon us. (1 John 4:16)

In the Kingdom of God there is no such thing as retirement, at least the bible makes no mention of anyone retiring.

If your friends ask you if your doctor says you have a certain disease, you reply, "Yes, but I am saying by Jesus' stripes I am healed in accordance to First Peter 2:24." (Isaiah 53:4-5; Matthew 8:17)

The nations that refuse to serve God will lose their power to be world leaders. (Isaiah 60:12) Politically, they will be like a nation that does not get enough rain to feed their population.

Preachers, were you anointed by a person to be a preacher, or were you anointed by the same one who anointed Jesus to be a preacher? (Luke 4:18)

Imagine a sign hanging above the front door of your home that says NO FEAR HERE. (John 14:27)

God is pro-choice where your own life is concerned, not where the life of someone else is concerned. (Deuteronomy 30:19) However, he admonishes us to choose life rather than death.

Don't be misled by the word "holy" in the bible. It just means to be set apart for a specific function. God is holy because he has set himself apart so he can function as God.

Woe unto those that call evil good, and good evil;
those that love darkness more than light. (Isaiah 5:20)

When Jesus found people walking in darkness,
he became their light. (John 1:4)

The purpose of God's army is not to conquer,
but to set free those who have been conquered by
Satan's deception. (Romans 8:36-39; John 14:27)

If you want to train a horse, the first thing you have
to do is get his attention. If you want to train people
to be obedient to God, the first thing you have to
do is get their attention. Miracles that only God
can do will get their attention. (John 2:23, 3:2)

Before the Israelites got to their Promised Land, they had to go through a wilderness. This might also befall us before we reach our Promised Land (Exodus 16:32)

Some people feel more comfortable with a lie than with the truth. A lie can be tailored to match their mood or their preconceived ideas.

We don't have to be perfect to serve God, but we do need to make a commitment to make a determined effort to serve him perfectly.

To be obedient to God, we must be able to hear his voice, either directly or from the bible.
(Matthew 4:4)

If you believe you never make mistakes, check the erasers on your lead pencils to see it they have been used.

Jesus=word=truth=life=light=bread=peace=resurrection=God (John 6:33)

There is a difference between a movement and an institution. The church started as a movement. It was called THE WAY. (Acts 24:14) If the movement stops moving, it will become an institution, maybe it already has.

You can't steer something that is not moving. If the church is not moving, it does not need to be steered.

Anyone who says they love God, but hates people is a liar. He who does not love those that he can see, cannot love a God that he can't see. (1 John 4:20)

God's army is made up of volunteers. No one is forced to join. (Psalms 110:3)

The day will come when the glory of God will cover the earth as the waters cover the sea. (Habakkuk 2:14)

A true leader does not quit when he makes mistakes. He learns from his mistakes, and continues to lead.

If we exchange yokes with Jesus, we find rest. Why? Because his yoke is not as heavy as our yoke. (Matthew 11:30)

Church leaders who work themselves into an early grave because they rely on man's power rather than God's power don't become martys because they caused their own death. (Psalms 46:10) Even Jesus did not begin his ministry until he was empowered by God's Spirit. (Luke 4:18)

When you hear a loud sound from a trumpet
that does not stop, that will signal the end
of the world. (1 Corinthians 15:52-55)

Don't harden your heart when you are criticized.
Weigh the criticism in your mind to see if
any part of it might be accurate. This would
be an act of wisdom. (Psalms 95:8-11)

John the Baptist preached repentance to prepare
the people for Jesus' first coming. We will
need to preach repentance to prepare people
for Jesus' second coming. (2 Peter 3:9-14)

Without patience we will probably never
acquire enough faith to have an experience
like those at Pentecost. (Acts 2:1-4)

Members of the early church talked so much
about God anointing people that they became
known as the Anointed Ones; or if you prefer
Greek, they were called Christians. (Acts 11:26)

Every society needs rules, but rules can never be
a substitute for personal discipline. Without it the
people will need a policeman to enforce the rules.
This could result in a police state if a significant
number of people lack personal discipline.

If you are praying and still drowning, maybe your prayers are too long. It is not the length of a prayer that gets results, it is the depth of the prayer. (Matthew 14:30)

The path of those who are in right standing with God is like the light of dawn, which shines brighter and brighter until there is full light. (Proverbs 4:18)

Woe unto those who seek counseling from someone other than God. (Isaiah 30:1)

If you can't get along with your earthly Dad, try your heavenly Dad. He said he would be a father to the fatherless. (Psalms 68:5)

As wonderful as God's miracles are, they are not as wonderful as having your name written in the Book of Life. (Luke 10:20; Revelation 17:8, 22:19)

God's Spirit is available to be our covering. (Isaiah 30:1)

God is not only a God of order, he is the God of our disorder, if we have committed ourselves to be his servants. He knows we are not going to do everything accurately, but our commitment to him must be total, even if our actions contain flaws. (Matthew 24:45-46)

Some people think if they don't admit how great
they are, that makes them humble. Humility
involves our thinking, also. (Proverbs 23:7)

You cannot over evil with evil. You overcome
evil with good. (Romans 12:21)

Every belief we have will have a consequence,
whether for good or for bad. Our body
will go where our beliefs take it.

When we pray to God, we come into his
presence. When we praise God, he comes
into our presence. (Psalms 22:3)

It is easy to trust God when everything is going our
way, but God expects us to continue to trust him
regardless of our circumstances. (Deuteronomy 8:2-6)

In God's kingdom everything works by love. Not goose
bump love, but love based on a vow.
(1 Corinthians 13:1-13)

It may seem like a burden for us to take up
our cross daily. But life is daily, as well as
nightly. The Devil never sleeps. While we are
sleeping, he is planning his next attack. But
God doesn't sleep either. (Psalms 121:4)

If someone is at a higher level than you, don't become
jealous. Rather, use it as a motivation to cause you
to work harder, so you can go to a higher level.

If you have been assigned to dig a ditch, dig the
best ditch anyone has ever seen. You will not
have to brag, the ditch will speak for you.

When we believe that Jesus is who he says he is,
and that he has done what the bible says he has
done, we are born into the Kingdom of God. But
we attain maturity by growth, by progression. Here
are the steps to growth: believe (Romans 10:10),
disciple (Matthew 10:24), servant (Matthew 25:21),
friend (John 15:15), son or daughter (John 1;12).

God has promised to reward those who
are obedient to him. (Hebrews 11:6)

Faith in God pleases God even when what you are
trying to do fails. Being willing to make the effort
to try to succeed is proof of your faith, not the final
results, which may be a colossal failure. (Hebrews 11:6)

When people in the bible asked Jesus a
question, he would address their problem
rather than their question if their question
did not involve their problem. (John 8:19)

Do you want to really hurt the Devil? You can
hurt him the same way you hurt God: Don't
do what he tells you to do. If the Devil tells
you to get revenge against someone, don't get
revenge. This will break the Devil's heart.

Preachers may judge their success by how many
new members they add to the church roll. God
judges success by the accuracy of the preacher's
preaching of the Kingdom of God, which may
result in the loss of church members. (John 6:66)

If your heart is right with God, whatever breaks
your heart breaks God's heart. (Luke 4:18)

The more we give of ourselves to God, the more we
can receive from God. (Matthew 11:28; John 14:27)

God does not object to his servants being fanatical as long
as they are obedient to follow his voice. (Romans 10:2)

God said he would spew out of his mouth luke
warm christians. So, if you are a luke warm
christian, don't be surprised when he spews
you out of his mouth. (Revelation 3:16)

When Israel left Egypt, they came to the Red
Sea. God said to Moses, "Go forward." The sea

had not yet parted. He went forward by faith in God's word, then the sea parted. (Exodus 14:15)

Some think God is a long way off, but he is only a prayer away. (Philippians 4:6)

Those that strive for mastery must be temperate, self-controlled, in all things. (1 Corinthians 9:25)

If you commit yourself to serve God, you are no longer your own, to do only what pleases you.

A binge of 1,000 calories begins with one nibble.

If your outgo exceeds your income, your upkeep will be your downfall.

What is the greatest type of love? It is the kind were you are willing to lay down your life for someone. (John 15:13)

There must be a reason why the bible emphasizes that the God referred to in the bible is one God, not many gods. Some people apparently believed there were many gods. There may be some that still believe that.

What is worse than finding a worm in the apple you are eating? Finding one-half of a worm.

Our hurts by others usually go much deeper
than we think they do. That is why we must
be quick to forgive. The longer we wait,
the more damage the hurts will do.

If your commitment to serve God is solid, the
times you fail will discourage you, but they will
not devastate you. (2 Corinthians 4:8-9)

Don't forget to forgive yourself as well
as others, even those you hate.

The hardest person to conquer is
yourself. (Romans 7:15)

Regardless of how strong our commitment
is to serve God, our flesh is weak and subject
to attacks by Satan. (Luke 22:31)

If you are full of pride, you are
automatically under Satan's control.

The purpose for joining a church by a
confession of faith in Jesus is not to have
a social life but to have eternal life.

Your tongue is your biggest asset and your biggest
liability, depending upon how you use it. God

created the world with his tongue (his words). He said what he created was good. If anything goes awry, we can correct it with our words, because we are made in his image. God gave us authority like he has. (Genesis 1:28; Proverbs 6:2, 18:21)

The bible tells us that God's servants should say continually, "Let God be magnified, who takes pleasure in the prosperity of his servants." (Psalms 35:27)

Who is the true God? He is the one who is faithful to keep his covenant. He is merciful toward those that love him and obey his commandments. He is faithful to keep his covenant for a thousand generations. (Deuteronomy 7:9)

Since the fall of Adam and Eve in the Garden of Eden, mankind does not know how to love. He has to be taught. God is the teacher; through his written word and his Holy Spirit. (Genesis 6:5; John 13:34-35, 14:26)

One way to lose your sanity is not have a buddy. Prisoners of war who are isolated will make friends with spiders and mice that come into their cells, so they can maintain their sanity.

9

Church leaders need to be on guard to keep church services from becoming like a spectator sport.

Parents, when your children do something that breaks your heart, don't give up on them. God didn't give up on you when you broke his heart.

Put some chocolate on your sin, then it won't taste like sin anymore. This is what you do when you make an excuse for your sin.

We should think of the bible as God's love letter to us. Although God was sorely displeased when Adam and Eve disobeyed him, he never gave up on them.

It sounds illogical, but peace sometimes comes after a struggle, not instead of a struggle.

You may have problems due to what people have done to you in the past, but you can choose not to let it adversely affect your future. You will also need to forgive them.

Theologians, if you are going to teach and preach theology, you need to be able to converse with Theo (God) as a friend talks to a friend. (Exodus 33:11)

You determine how deep you want to go in your relationship with God.

Growing old is not so bad when you consider the only other alternative.

It is sad when Satan believes in God and trembles before people believe in God and tremble.
(James 2:19)

The Kingdom of God does not just involve works, but words that have power. (1 Corinthians 4:20)

Preachers, if you are preaching a comfortable religion, you are not preaching what Jesus preached.
(1 Corinthians 2:16; Matthew 5:11, 44)

People you refuse to forgive will not lose any sleep because you refused to forgive them, but you will.

In Old Testament days, God used people's fears of him to force them to be obedient to him. In the New Testament era, it is God's goodness that draws people to him. But God's goodness has to be demonstrated by his servants if the world is going to experience his goodness. (Romans 2:4)

Withholding your forgiveness from someone who hurt you will not cause them to suffer, it will cause you to lose your peace.

Have you noticed in the bible when God tells one of his servants to do something, he never asks them if it is convenient for them to do what he tells them to do?

Satan is crazy, but he is not stupid. He is a master in deceiving people, and he probably knows more scripture than you do. He will try to use it against you, just like he used it against Jesus. (Matthew 4:6)

God desires to show his sons and daughters to the world, but we must be obedient and willing to be like Jesus when he was on the earth. (John 14:12)

God wants us to remind him of his promises, but it is not because he doesn't remember them. It is because we have to remember them in order to remind him. Isn't God wise? (Isaiah 43:26)

A word of wisdom to those who are planning to get married: If you want a marriage made in heaven, you need to get God involved in selecting someone to marry. Yes, God will help you find a suitable mate. Not perfect, but suitable. There is no such thing as a perfect mate.

To whom much has been given, from them much will be required. (Luke 12:48)

Your actions will probably speak louder than your words. But words are essential because they initiate your actions, they tell your body what to do.

How different would your life be if you set your affections on things that are of heaven rather than the things on the earth? (Colossians 3:2)

If you lack wisdom, ask God for wisdom. He gives wisdom liberally. But ask in faith, without any hidden motives for wanting wisdom. (James 1:5-6)

Would we be fearless and stronger if we believed that God is with us? (Joshua 1:9)

Worshipping religion is more comfortable than worshipping God. Religion doesn't talk back. It doesn't correct us.

Having faith in God is just as important as obeying his commandments. (Revelation 14:12)

Blessed are those who die because they are being obedient in serving God. (Revelation 14:13)

As powerful as God is and could use his power to do anything, yet he has chosen to use his power to do good. (Matthew 10:7-8)

The portion of the bible written by God through his servants is addressed to our spirit, not our physical being. Our physical being will view the bible as foolishness. (1 Corinthians 2:14)

God wants his servants to be kings and priests in the spiritual realm. (Revelation 1:6) So, if you are his servant, expect him to crown you. He will crown you with loving kindness and tender mercies.
(Psalms 103:4)

When you have a friendship with someone who operates in the supernatural power of God, your friendship will be supernatural.

God's Spirit, sometimes referred to in the bible as Holy Spirit, wants to be your close friend, your bosom buddy. (John 1:18, 13:23; Luke 16:22; Jeremiah 32:18; Isaiah 40:11; Proverbs 18:24)

When you are committed to God halfheartedly, you are like a man with one foot in the grave and the other foot on a banana peeling.

America was not built by perfect people, but much of its constitution appears to be modeled in accordance with what is written in the bible. Its leaders were not ashamed to quote the bible, or call the nation to prayer and fasting when it was in deep trouble.

To please God, knowing the will of God is the first step. Being in the will of God is the second step.

Some things defy wisdom. Why is it when you hurt yourself and people laugh, the hurt is worse?

If we accept Jesus as our savior and our boss, he will grant us the power of attorney to use his name.
(Psalms 124:8; Mark 16:17-18; Acts 4:16-17)

Alcoholic beverages will bite like a serpent, and cause you to speak perverse things.
(Proverbs 23:31-33)

You need wisdom to discern between an elegant sermon and a bible based sermon. Both can be appealing. (Romans 16:18)

What would cause someone to feel more joy with their pet than they feel with God?

A mark of your character is how well you get along with people you don't like.

The true God is a God of peace. He does not force anyone to worship him. However, he will fight if he is challenged or his servants are abused. (Isaiah 49:25)

Do you know why a humming bird hums? It is because he does not remember the words to the song he is singing.

God's plan is that we not only serve him, but we serve each other. This will reduce the strife that people have with each other. (Galatians 5:13; Philippians 2:3; Hebrews 12:28)

Love with a hidden agenda is not true love. At some point in time, the hidden agenda must come to the surface.

To impact our minds, the bible contrasts evil with darkness, and good with light. If you walk in the dark, you can't see where you are going to end up. You might be shocked when you see your destination.

> If you always search for wisdom, wisdom will accumulate. And you will eventually be promoted. (Proverbs 4:5-8)

> The best way to glorify God is to do something glorious in his name, such as a miracle. (Matthew 25:29-31; Luke 13:11-13)

> If you chase after personal pleasure, pleasure could become your God.

To know the truth, you have to know God's words, because God's words contain the truth. (John 17:17)

> If you follow Jesus, you will find others who are following him.

> Love, the God kind of love, is something that we should pursue. It can be used as a weapon to defeat hate. (Matthew 5:43-44)

One of the common mistakes made by those who want to be God's servant is to substitute religious ritual for an intimate relationship with God. (John 10:27)

A true leader does not quit when he makes a mistake.
He learns from his mistake and keeps going.

To qualify for God's authority for ourselves, we have
to have God's love as the foundation for our lives.

If you don't feel free, it is because you don't
know God's truth. (John 8:31-32)

Could your faith in God be more
valuable than gold? (1 Peter 1:7)

Our faith in God is tested by patience. (James 1:3-4)

The Kingdom of God is not just another kingdom.
Those in the Kingdom of God do not take sides,
they take over. They do not debate, they deliver
people from Satan's deception. They demonstrate the
power of the Kingdom of God. (1 Corinthians 2:4)

Preachers, if you cannot steer your congregation
in the direction you want it to go, maybe
your congregation is not moving. You can't
steer something that is not moving.

It is somewhat scary when you realize that others
need to know what you know in order to survive and
prosper. It is especially scary when you realize that

others need to know what you know to stay out of hell, and you will be held accountable if you don't tell them.

Adam, the first man that God created, was given authority over the whole earth. With authority comes responsibilities and constant vigilance. (1 Peter 5:8)

You cannot make informed choices if you are not informed. The best way to stay informed is to read the bible and other informative material.

An emotion out of control can be as dangerous as a wild horse.

God's peace in our life is not due to the absence of war. We can have God's peace even while we are in the middle of a war. (John 14:27)

Where do you find joy when there is nothing in your life to be joyful about? Jesus will share his joy with you through his words. Buy a bible with Jesus' words in red letters, and read the red. (Nehemiah 8:10; John 16:24)

During his earthly ministry, Jesus said he did not come to be served but to serve. He cannot serve us if we are not willing to be served. (John 13:5-8; Luke 22:27)

If you don't forgive people, you will not be able to love them as Jesus commanded. (John 15:17)

If you have a problem forgiving people, it might be because you won't receive forgiveness for yourself. If you feel like you have to earn God's forgiveness, you will require people to earn your forgiveness. Freely you have received, freely give. (Matthew 10:8)

Unforgiveness is a trap that even the wise might fall into. (Colossians 3:13)

Jesus will be to you a stumbling stone or a solid rock you can build your house on. The choice is yours. (Romans 9:33)

Be aware of this progression in emotions: Unfulfilled expectations lead to a feeling of offense. Offense leads to anger. Anger leads to hate. Hate leads to violence.

A person whose roots are in God's word is like a fruit tree by a stream of water, whose roots go deep and are nourished by the water of the stream to bring forth fruit. (Psalms 1:3)

10

When traveling life's highway, don't look back toward the errors that are behind you. Just repent of those errors and keep traveling in hope. Don't recall constantly in your mind the former things.
(Isaiah 43:18-19)

A wise person will say, "When I die, bury me deep beneath the sod, but leave my tongue free so I can praise my God." (Psalms 111:10)

Don't dwell on problems. Dwell on the solution to the problems.

Pray to receive a "discerning" spirit, so you can evaluate what is driving the people that have a controversy with you.

Sometimes we are not choosing between
good and bad, we are choosing between
good and best, what is important and what
is most important. (Luke 10:38-42)

We would be wise to examine the food we eat.
A lot of chemicals are used in processing food.
Would you rather have an egg laid by a hen
or an egg laid by a chemist? Read labels. Read
labels. Read labels, says the voice of wisdom.

We will probably never fully understand
God, but we can still fully trust him, because
he is trustworthy. (Psalms 125:1)

There are many instances in the bible where people
gathered to talk and debate, but the person who
could perform miracles carried the day. (John 2:23)

Some people believe God does foolish things.
The foolishness of God is wiser than the
wisdom of men. (Corinthians 1:25)

God is not only a singer, he is the
chief singer. (Habakkuk 3:1,19)

Would you believe that God hurts when he
sees you hurting? (Hebrews 4:15-16)

Ask God what is on his heart. Don't be surprised if he, in turn, asks you what is on your heart.
(Jeremiah 29:11)

Remember, there is no vaccine that protects us from a broken heart, so choose your friends wisely. (Proverbs 16:20, 28:26)

Stay busy helping others, and you won't have time to get depressed. There are a lot of needy people in the world. (Acts 20:35)

Husbands and wives honor your marriage vows, whether you feel like it or not. You will experience the power of an honored vow. (Ecclesiastes 5:4)

When you get serious about your relationship with God, don't be surprised if you hear these words going over and over in your mind: Be obedient. Be obedient. Be obedient. (2 Corinthians 2:9)

Your spirit may want to serve God, but your flesh doesn't. (Matthew 26:41)

Have you ever thought of yourself as a jewel? Would it surprise you to know that God thinks of you as a Jewel if you have committed yourself to serve him. (Malachi 3:17)

God's love toward us is unconditional, but that doesn't mean it doesn't have a purpose. (John 3:16)

God expects his servants to reign as kings, but their crown is different from earthly kings. God's servants are crowned with God's glory, honor, loving kindness and tender mercies. (Psalms 8:4-6, 25:6)

When the church was first formed, the members were laughing so hard, those outside the church accused them of being drunk. (Acts 2:1-13)

If hell is a real place, you would be wise to avoid going there. (Acts 2:21-41)

If the oceans roar with God glory, why can't we? (1 Chronicles 16:32)

Judge yourself, then God won't need to judge you. (1 Corinthians 11:31)

If you are in covenant with God or a person, it is very important that you remain faithful to that covenant. (2 Timothy 2:12-13)

Sometimes inspiration comes because of perspiration, because of hard work.

Wisdom is more valuable than gold,
and understanding more valuable
than silver. (Proverbs 16:16)

Whosoever rewards evil, evil will not depart
from his house. (Proverbs 17:13)

Men, if you did not receive glory because you had
an irresponsible father, accept God as your father
and he will restore your glory. (Psalms 51:10-12)

How do you react when your preacher stops
preaching and starts meddling in your life. If he
is telling the truth, do you have a right to ignore
him? Would you be wise not to ignore him?

There is no price great enough to cause a
fool to seek wisdom, seeing he does not
have a heart for it. (Proverbs 17:16)

Waiting on God will test your patience.
(Psalms 25:5) When God opens a door, no one
can shut it. This will test your patience.

God has made you uniquely you. However,
you can learn what others know as long as you
separate the good from the bad they know.

When we have a personal encounter with God, we will feel unworthy. This is our confirmation that we have had a personal encounter with God.

Hell is a special type of pain. It is not like the pain from an injury, which usually subsides with time. Hell is like being injured repeatedly. A more accurate description of hell would be torture, but you can't see who is torturing you because it is pitch dark. You can't ask anyone, because you are all alone.

When you have a full revelation of how bad hell is, you will not want anyone to go there, not even your worst enemy. You will pray for the salvation of your worst enemy.

If you don't like being alone forever, that would be another good reason to avoid going to hell.

Pose this question to Jews who don't believe Jesus is their Messiah (Anointed One). "How will you recognize your Messiah when he comes?" If they don't know, ask them this question. "If you don't know how to recognize him, is it possible that he has already come but you didn't recognize him?"

Knowing about Jesus' miracles during his earthly ministry will help you build your faith for miracles if you believe Jesus' words that his followers can do what he did. (John 14:12) You also need to believe what Jesus said about those that Jesus' disciples converted. (John 17:20)

You will know you have arrived at the very threshold of the Kingdom of God when you have accepted God as your beloved. (2 Thessalonians 2:13)

If you expect God to fight on your side, you must be connected to him permanently, because you don't advance until the battle begins.

Two men can be brothers in the natural realm, and still not be brothers in the spiritual realm. To be brothers in the spiritual realm, they must have the same spiritual father, either God or Satan. This is why Jesus did not refer to every Jew as his brother, even though they had a common ancestry. (John 8:44)

God doesn't merely dislike pride, he hates it. God can love you and still hate what is destroying you. (Proverbs 8:13)

The abominable will not be allowed into heaven. (Revelation 21:8) An abominable person in God's eyes is someone who says they know God but their actions deny him.

If you have made a commitment to serve God,
there is no such thing as a private life.

You would be wise not to wait until you get to hell
before you repent of your sins. If there is a door
out of hell, how are you going to find it in the
dark? Hell is so dark, you can feel the darkness.

Homosexuality was not Sodom's sin. It was
the end result of their sin. Their sin was pride,
fullness of bread, an abundance of idleness, and
failure to help the needy. (Ezekiel 16:49)

There is a difference in spending money and
investing money. Money spent is gone forever. Money
invested will come back to you, either as money or
something in which you need to invest more money.

Our goal should be to have enough wisdom to
know how to please God, and what type of legacy
to leave our children and grand-children.

Some people believe it is a sin not to worry about
problems. They believe you don't care, you don't have
sympathy. The basis for worry is fear, and the bible tells
us not to fear. Fear must be replaced by faith in God's
ability and willingness to help us with our problems.

God is not asking us to fully understand him, but he is asking us to fully trust him, because he is trustworthy.

> The bible describes God's Spirit as a flowing stream. We can't control a flowing stream. When we get in it, we go wherever it goes.

> Have you heard about the man who was thankful for bad luck? He said if it wasn't for bad luck, he wouldn't have any luck at all.

> A half-truth is the same as a whole lie.

If your desire is for certain people to go to hell, how could God be pleased with that? (Luke 9:54-56)

The proof of the pudding is in the eating. Taste the Lord and you will know he is good. (Psalms 34:8)

> Some people refuse to take responsibility for their disobedience toward God. They want to blame it on someone else. (Genesis 3:1-13)

> The best way to show our loyalty to Jesus is to feed his sheep (his followers). What do we feed them, Jesus' teachings. (John 6:63)

Our God is a picky God. He will hold us accountable for even idle words that we speak. (Matthew 12:36)

If you see God through the lens of self condemnation, that should encourage you rather than discourage you. Keep looking. You will eventually find the place where you need to repent. (Acts 2:37-38)

Don't be surprised if your relationship with God goes through phases. From disdain to curiosity to tolerance to wonder to partial acceptance as your boss to asking for favors for yourself and others, to thankfulness, to love, to addiction for him. At any point along the journey you can experience a dry spell, when God seems to be totally absent. These will be times of testing.

If we are so minded, we can usually find an excuse for being offended rather than forgiving.

One of the problems with life is that it is so daily.

If we fail to forgive, Satan will have an advantage over us. (2 Corinthians 2:10-11)

God did not recommend that we be of good courage, he commanded it. (Joshua 1:9) Joshua was preparing for a battle when God spoke this to him. However, he assured Joshua that he would be with him in combat. (Joshua 1:5)

It is not accurate to say, "The Devil is in the details." The Devil doesn't care what you do as long as you don't worship God.

Don't be deceived about what Satan looks like. He does not wear a red suit, or have horns, or have a pointed tail or carry a pitch fork. Satan is a spirit, an angel that tried to overthrow God.

You never know where a woodpecker is going to peck. The bible characterizes fallen angels as birds. You don't know in advance where a demon spirit will attack you. (Revelation 18:2)

If you have made a commitment to serve God, ask him at the end of each day if you have spoken any words during the day that grieved him.

Jesus is God's right hand man.
(Mark 16:19; Acts 7:55-56)

To prepare for our next life, we need to start now. The world will come to an end without any advance warning, or we could die in an accident.

He that sins against wisdom sins against his own soul.
Those that hate wisdom, love death. (Proverbs 8:1,36)

> Give instructions to a wise man and he
> will become wiser. (Proverbs 9:9)

> By wisdom, the days of your life will
> be multiplied, and the years of your life
> shall be increased. (Proverbs 9:1,11)

Even brothers can differ in their wisdom. A man who was always broke asked his brother why he always had money. Here is the brother's answer: When you see something you like, you buy it if you can. When I see something I like, I do without it if I can.

> Love is not always a good thing, especially if
> you love spiritual darkness more than light
> because your deeds are evil. (John 3:19)

They say that money talks, but you have to be able to keep it long enough to start a conversation.

> If you want to renew your youth, forgive
> those who trespass against you, who bad
> mouth you, who abuse you, etc.

Married couples take a vow to love each other as long as they live, not as long as they feel like it.

If your mouth is out of control, your body is out of control. Your body will go wherever your mouth takes it.

A famous wise man said, "If we have no friends, we have no pleasure."

God rewards us when we are diligent in our worship of him, because diligence signifies sincerity.

If you are deceived, you are living a lie.

Raising someone from the dead is a temporary miracle, because they will eventually die again and stay dead. Raising someone from spiritual death is a permanent miracle.

According to the bible, there are two types of light, light in the physical world and light in the spiritual world. We know when the light is physical, but we don't always know when it is spiritual. As strange as it may seem, spiritual light involves words. (John 6:63) One of Jesus' other names is the WORD OF GOD, because he is the light of the spiritual world. (John 1:1,14; Revelation 19:13)

Epilogue

This book includes God's wisdom and the world's wisdom, but the primary purpose for the book is to exalt God and his wisdom. In the course of writing this book, I heard these from God, "Your pen is your pulpit." So, I took very seriously what I wrote in this book.

I hope you take these WORDS OF WISDOM seriously also. My hope is that you will grab these words of wisdom and run with them.

The bible compares speaking words to sowing seeds. In the parable of the sower in the bible, we are apt to focus on the type of ground mentioned, but notice the sower (Jesus) sowed good seed in all types of ground. So, our job as sowers is to sow seed in all types of ground. We cannot tell in advance which soil will respond to the seeds sown.

Remember, just because a person has ears does not mean he has ears that are willing to hear. But we have to assume everyone has a hearing ear, and continue to sow seeds.

The words of wisdom in this book are only a portion of the wisdom you will receive from reading the bible for yourself. I strongly urge you to set aside a minimum of thirty minutes of your day to read the bible. To do this, you will probably have to forsake one of your favorite TV shows, but it will be worth it. Try it for one month and then you will know if it is worth it.

If you are new at reading the bible, I suggest that you start with the book called JOHN. Then read the books of MATTHEW and MARK and LUKE. These four books cover the era of Jesus' ministry while he was on the earth.

Jesus is the grand subject of the NEW TESTAMENT portion of the bible, so concentrate your bible study primarily on the NEW TESTAMENT. However, wait on studying the book called REVELATION until you are well established in the other scriptures.

I have written a book that explains the book in the bible called REVELATION. The title of the book I wrote is THE BOOK OF REVELATION FROM ALPHA TO OMEGA. You should be able to find it wherever books are sold. If you don't find it on a shelf, ask them to order it for you.

www.ingramcontent.com/pod-product-compliance
Ingram Content Group UK Ltd.
Pitfield, Milton Keynes, MK11 3LW, UK
UKHW022209230426
12048UKWH00016BA/732